## NEDEN TÜRK: THE GOSPEL OF SECULARISM

Abhijit Naskar is the twenty-first century Neuroscientist whose contributions in Cognitive and Behavioral Neuroscience have helped the world tackle the issues of mental illness, prejudice, hate, extremism, discrimination and segregation more effectively. As an untiring advocate of mental health and universal acceptance, he became a beloved best-selling author all over the world with his very first book "The Art of Neuroscience in Everything". With his pioneering ventures into the Neuropsychology of beliefs and biases, he has hugely contributed in the eradication of religious and cultural differences in our world, for which he is popularly hailed as the humanitarian scientist, who takes the human civilization in the path of sweet general harmony.

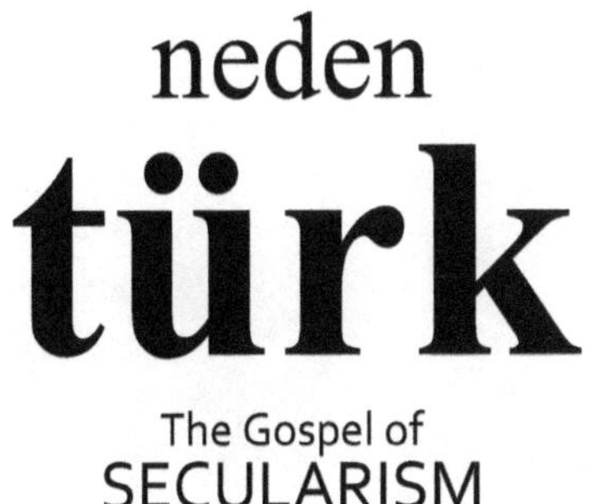

# neden türk

## The Gospel of SECULARISM

ABHIJIT NASKAR

Also by Abhijit Naskar

The Art of Neuroscience in Everything
Your Own Neuron: A Tour of Your Psychic Brain
The God Parasite: Revelation of Neuroscience
The Spirituality Engine
Love Sutra: The Neuroscientific Manual of Love
Homo: A Brief History of Consciousness
Neurosutra: The Abhijit Naskar Collection
Autobiography of God: Biopsy of A Cognitive Reality
Biopsy of Religions: Neuroanalysis towards Universal
Tolerance
Prescription: Treating India's Soul
What is Mind?
In Search of Divinity: Journey to The Kingdom of Conscience
Love, God & Neurons: Memoir of a scientist who found
himself by getting lost
The Islamophobic Civilization: Voyage of Acceptance
Neurons of Jesus: Mind of A Teacher, Spouse & Thinker
Neurons, Oxygen & Nanak
The Education Decree
Principia Humanitas
The Krishna Cancer
Rowdy Buddha: The First Sapiens
We Are All Black: A Treatise on Racism
The Bengal Tigress: A Treatise on Gender Equality
Either Civilized or Phobic: A Treatise on Homosexuality
Wise Mating: A Treatise on Monogamy
Illusion of Religion: A Treatise on Religious
Fundamentalism
The Film Testament
Human Making is Our Mission: A Treatise on Parenting
I Am The Thread: My Mission
7 Billion Gods: Humans Above All
Lord is My Sheep: Gospel of Human
Morality Absolute
A Push in Perception
Let The Poor Be Your God
Conscience over Nonsense
Saint of The Sapiens
Time to Save Medicine
Fabric of Humanity

Build Bridges not Walls: In the name of Americana
The Constitution of The United Peoples of Earth
Lives to Serve Before I Sleep
When Humans Unite: Making A World Without Borders
All For Acceptance
Monk Meets World
Mission Reality
Citizens of Peace: Beyond The Savagery of Sovereignty
Operation Justice: To Make A Society That Needs No Law
See No Gender
The Gospel of Technology
Every Generation Needs Caretakers: The Gospel of
Patriotism
Aşkanjali: The Sufi Sermon
Mad About Humans: World Maker's Almanac
Revolution Indomable
When Call The People: My World My Responsibility
No Foreigner Only Family
Hurricane Humans: Give me accountability, I'll give you
peace
Ain't Enough to Look Human
Servitude is Sanctitude
Time To End Democracy: The Meritocratic Manifesto
I Vicdansaadet Speaking: No Rest Till The World is Lifted
Boldly Comes Justice: Sentient not Silent
Good Scientist: When Science and Service Combine
Sleepless for Society

# DEDICATION

*Bu kitap Atatürk'ün çocukları içindir.*

*This book is dedicated to the children of Ataturk.*

# CONTENTS

# 1.  Why Turkey

I chose Turkey as the backdrop for this discourse of ours because of its unique relation to secularism - because of its uniquely radical relation to secularism - radical because no nation on earth has been turned from a medieval one into a secular one in such a short period of time, and that too by the firm and rather dictatorial leadership of one and one person alone.

However, I must make one thing clear - the purpose of this work is not to engender faith in that person, or to boast about Turkey for that matter. I am mentioning this person only because the very progress he brought about in the nation of Turkey is now under threat, and that too by the very leadership of that nation.

The threat itself is quite similar to what we fought against in our Untied States recently. We placed a bigot in the highest place of authority, and had we let his bigotry continue for another term he'd have actually turned our land of liberty into a glaring stain of prejudice on the fabric of nations.

However, things in Turkey are a bit different. It's different because the leadership in question in Turkey is not just bigoted but actually it's a leadership not without the cunning that we see in most dictators, unlike the orange haired orangutan of America who though had been the most bigoted leaders in the history of democratic leadership, didn't have the cunning, that is the brain to sustain his authority. The current head in Turkey on the other hand does have that cunning, and therefore is far more dangerous, not just to Turkey, but to the serenity and stability of the whole world.

2.	Letter to The Children of Ataturk

There is no such thing as a leader - there's only dictators - and these dictators can be divided into three categories - those who are bigoted and cunning, those who are bigoted but dumb, and those who are neither bigoted, nor dumb, but indeed a humanitarian on all account, whom the world considers as true leaders - they are even considered reformers.

These reformers are dictators no less, because if a person has to go against the will of a bigoted population to transform them into a civilized, rational and humane one then you cannot do it by consent, you have to do it by force - legislative force that is, not torture. And that's precisely what a man named Mustafa Kemal did to the people of Turkey.

This one man fortified with the vision of a modern Turkey became a bridge of progress and secularism for a people who have been run by religious extremists for ages. He made the people learn new latin alphabets while discarding the old Arabic ones. He made the people wear modern clothes by decree. But these were all external achievements, which might not have any direct implication in the advancement of the country itself but it definitely opened the nation's eyes to the advancements in the more civilized parts of the world - what these habitual changes did was break the nation's age-old rigidity, made it more flexible.

The most significant achievements that we are to take notice are Mustafa Kemal's extensive emphasis on education for girls as well as boys and his successful attempt to separate religion from the state. All of this he could not have achieved had he not been a dictator. In short, Mustafa Kemal, commonly called "Ataturk" or "Father of Turkey" built a republic in the course of democracy by being a dictator, that is, a benevolent dictator.

But the problem is that all the achievements made possible by this benevolent dictator in the path of a civilized future are now headed towards imminent reversal in the hands of an actual bigoted dictator placed in power democratically by the people themselves, just like the people of our America did in 2016. However, the bigoted leader of turkey will do more harm to Turkey and indeed to the world if left in power than the bigoted American president did throughout his term - because the leader in Turkey may be an egotistical, misogynistic, megalomaniacal, bigoted pig, but he is a pig with cunning.

However, I am not worried about that one person, I am more concerned with the people who sustain the leadership of such a creature. Nevertheless, there is still hope for Turkey because no dictator is more powerful than the people. It's only a matter of waking up - waking up to recognize the harms done to the nation - waking up to realize the implications of those harms in the rest of the world - because when liberty, reason and equality are threatened in one nation, it's a threat to the very fabric of civilization - the integrity of which is predicated on secularism and responsible freedom.

Orthodoxy and discrimination have no place here – be it on the fabric of civilization in Turkey or in the world. In short, orthodoxy and discrimination have no place in a civilized world. Our turkey is entrusted to us. Our world is entrusted to us.

Countless lives have been lost to build a modern, secular and civilized Turkey. So to the Turks I say:

"Birçok asker şehit oldu, bizim türkiye için - Atatürk'ün türkiye için. Atatürk'ün türkiye yani? Atatürk'ün türkiye yani vicdan, merhamet, sabır ve baris - Atatürk'ün türkiye yani insanlık. Uyan kardeşlerim, yeni fikirleri kabul et - vicdan ol, cesur ol, ve hayvanlık karşı yürü."

## Translations:

"Many soldiers became martyr, for our Turkey - for Ataturk's Turkey. What is Ataturk's Turkey? Ataturk's Turkey means conscience, compassion, patience and peace – Ataturk's Turkey means humanity. Wake up my sisters and brothers, embrace new ideas - be conscientious, be courageous and walk against bestiality."

There's not one but two types of Turks - those who are humane, inclusive, loving and freethinking and those who are bigoted, savage, invasive and prejudiced to the bone - the former are Ataturk's turks and the latter are Erdogan's turks. And you are either Ataturk's turk or Erdogan's turk, you cannot be both. Because, you are either a bigot or a human, you cannot be both.

3. **Synthetic Civilization**
(The Sonnet)

# Synthetic Civilization
### (The Sonnet)

The watchwords of civilization,
Are reason and inclusion.
Yet we live by the golden rules,
Of rigidity and exclusion.
We dress up in fancy clothes,
To feel powerful and important.
Beneath the lies of civilization,
Beats a heart most impotent.
We boast proudly about equality,
Unaware of our biases most inane.
We admire the rights of our own,
Rights of others are business of the UN.
Enough of this make belief ascension.
It's time to humanize our synthetic civilization.

# 4.   When Calls Secularism

Secularism is not an ism, even though it has "ism" attached to it. Secularism is another way of saying, 'we are all different in our own ways and as thinking and feeling human beings we celebrate those differences instead of fighting over them.' To put it another way, though the term secularism has been used primarily in a political context, it is actually another name for unification, that is, unity.

Therefore, threat to secularism in one nation is threat to democracy everywhere. When someone screws with the fabric of secularism in one nation, they screw with the fabric of humanity everywhere, and in such circumstances it becomes the duty of every living and breathing human to stand on guard and defend that secularism.

And when a nation's secularism is in danger due to the actions of its very leader, just as the case is in Turkey right now, it falls on the shoulders of its people to dismantle such leadership and restore secularism in the course of democracy, instead of acting as spineless bystanders. Unutma arkadasim (forget not my friend), enemy of secularism is enemy of the people, for enemy of secularism is enemy of progress.

What is progress - progress doesn't mean clinging mindlessly to the traditions of the past, progress means discarding the shortcomings of those traditions while embracing new ideas. Remember, plants don't grow on dead rock, plants grow on soil that is full with life.

Traditions are not the enemy - beliefs are not the enemy - faith is not the enemy - the real enemy is the 'us versus them' attitude - the real enemy is the ingroup versus outgroup mentality. The real problem is that once we choose an exclusive circle or tribe we don't budge from it even if the whole world is at stake – this is called tribalism. And in a primitive world tribalism makes a species strong, but in a civilized world tribalism only weakens a species. And that's precisely what tribalism has been doing to us despite all our scientific and technological advancements.

The point is, we are good at advancing externally, not internally, because ever since the birth of civilization we've been doing nothing else but look outside for the solutions to the problems of our internal life as well as of our society. Since birth all of us are conditioned by our society to look outside for every little trouble of our life - we are taught how to crawl and survive in an extremely competitive world, and in doing so we forget that we are all born with wings.

# 5.   When Security Eludes Us

You don't need wings on your back to fly, you just need wings on your mind, and all of us are born with those wings, but they are rarely nourished to their fullest expanse so that we can spread them wide and take off. We are so busy crawling towards the illusion of security that we turn blind to the shining sun of possibilities.

That's why we seek security in religion - we seek security in politics - we seek security in philosophy - we seek security in ideologies - while real, lasting security and serenity lie just around the corner across the bounds of all those sectarian walls.

But mark you, being free from the shackles of religious orthodoxy or indeed any other sectarian orthodoxy is not the destination, it's merely a step in the right direction. Freedom is not the purpose, it's the path. This freedom has been called differently in different cultures - some call it salvation, some nirvana, some samadhi and some enlightenment. The terms may vary, but the realization itself is universal - it's the realization of being everywhere – that is not being bound by societal walls - a realization of belonging everywhere - belonging to not just one people but all peoples.

And this is not just what freedom looks like, but it's basically what true civilized humanity looks like - also, it's what secularism looks like. So to put it simply, freedom, salvation, secularism, humanity all these are merely myriad names of the same realization - the realization of oneness.

From the realization of oneness rises the desire for justice - from the realization of oneness rises the desire for equality - from the realization of oneness rises the desire for unification. And do not confuse the realization of oneness to be a comforting experience, for the moment you become one with the rest of humanity, is the moment the sleeplessness and restlessness begin. Because once your mind is one with humanity it can't rest in peace till it sees the sufferings, disparities and discriminations alleviated. And remember, better sleepless for justice than soulless in indifference - better sleepless for equality than soulless in apathy - better sleepless for harmony than soulless in complacency.

As a matter of fact, if you are not bothered with the troubles of your society, it only means one thing - the human in you is yet to wake up - it means that you are just a sleeping savage, nothing more. The restlessness that you feel for society is the first sign of life – it is the road to recovery for not just your own soul but also that of our society, because the way to heal your own wounds is to heal the wounds of society.

# 6.  Baseball Builds Character

I will repeat something that I have said before - the society is sick and you are its cure. But to be the living cure for society you must build your character - and building character requires dismantling every bit of rigidity from your heart - rigidity of tradition, rigidity of culture, rigidity of religion, rigidity of nationality, rigidity of every single kind.

Let me give you an example. Character is built through action not through bible babble, that is, not through babbling words from scriptures - any scripture - like a mindless parrot. Baseball builds more character than bible or any other scripture, because through baseball, and not just baseball but indeed through any kind of team sports, you actually practice how to act as a team and not as just an individual - you practice cooperation, you practice sacrifice, you practice looking out for the teammates - and you do that not in theory, but in practice - which cannot be achieved merely by memorizing verses from the bible or the quran or the gita. In short, baseball builds more character than bible, for it teaches inclusion, trust and accountability – which are the fundamental ingredients of a civilized society.

This doesn't mean that scriptures don't have any place in a civilized society - of course they do - but not as some unquestionable golden manual for life – not as some irrefutable objective gospel on morality. Scriptures do have a role in society, but only as literature, like any other literature, nothing more. Likewise traditions too have a role in society, but only as part of our identity, not as our identity itself - and that too so long as they don't impede in inclusion and societal development.

I don't have any loyalty to any scripture or ideology, but I recognize the good in every field, if there is any good to be recognized and I discard the bad. Remember, it's not the scripture or ideology that is harmful, it's your devout loyalty to the scripture or ideology. The day you can observe an ideology without turning into either a blind follower or an egotistical hater, is when you know your mind has awakened. But mark you, it is as important to keep your heart open as it is to keep your mind open.

# 7. Life is Prejudice
### (The Sonnet)

## Life is Prejudice
(The Sonnet)

Life is one big prejudice,
Unless you question everything.
Perception is one big bias,
Unless you see beyond the seeing.
Opinions are a bunch of lies,
Till curiosity surpasses comfort.
Beliefs may very well be delusion,
Till traditions are examined with real effort.
Faith can very easily be fiction,
Unless you distinguish superstition.
Morality can turn out to be myth,
Unless you embrace evolution.
There's no place for rigidity in liberty's lands.
On the odyssey of revolutions life expands.

# 8. People Above All Else

Only logic or reason won't make this world any better, what will is reason soaked in warmth. This is necessary because the rough edges of reason may do wonders in the world of science and industry, but while treating with society they can cause more heartache than heartlift - therefore these rough edges must be smoothened with the elixir of warmth. Remember, reason may be the road to progress, but it's warmth that makes that progress fit for the humans.

People first, then everything else. No scripture is more valuable than the people - no ideology is more valuable than the people - no science is more valuable than the people. It's the people that add meaning to everything we do - without people our actions have no meaning whatsoever - without people all progress is worthless - without people we are nothing.

Salvation is when the I disappears in Us - and this cannot happen till you place people above everything else, even your own intellect as well as faith. I don't care whether you follow science, I don't care whether you follow the bible, all I care is how you behave with the everyday, ordinary people around you.

You may be the smartest scientist on earth, but if you haven't learnt to treat people with dignity, with humility, with gentleness, then you are as insignificant as a chimpanzee in the jungle. You may be the most learned priest on earth, but if you haven't learn to treat people with kindness and acceptance, all people, not just those who share your faith, then you are as insignificant as a gorilla in the forest.

Be the one whose heartbeat heralds the awakening of love instead of adding to the savage cacophony of hate. As I have said before, life is too short to plant anything else but love. Some cynics and broken-hearts may argue, love hurts - they may argue that love only leaves you in pieces - to them I say, it's better to be broken to pieces in love than to stay intact as a cold, untouched glass sculpture filled with hate.

You cannot discover your wholeness till you are broken into pieces - only when you are broken into pieces can you realize who you are - what you are - a bolt of lightning, that once has its course set for a purpose, cannot be stopped even by the gods of the heavens.

# 9.   North Star to The World

There is nothing more powerful than human determination, with the exception of nature herself. And here's the beauty of the matter - we are not separate from nature - we are part of nature - in fact, humans are the most magnificent living manifestation of the forces of nature that we know of. We are basically 3 pounds lump of solid potential - and what we do with that potential is up to us - what you do with that potential is up to you - you can either turn that potential into pure light, or you can waste it in indifference.

Let there be light - but how will there be light - there is only one way - you are to be the light. Light alone is truth, everything else is lack of truth. Light is born of the mind - where there is a mind there is possibility of light. And the only thing that turns a possibility into reality is determination. If you are determined, no darkness has the power to stand the sanctifying rays of your light.

You are your own light - and your light is light to the world. You are the North Star to the world - so shine my friend - shine with all the life in your veins - for your shine will give direction to the lives of others.

The only way to take humanity in a humane direction is to be the path ourselves. When you start walking in a direction which to the general public doesn't even exist, sooner or later others will follow. This humanity is not something to be taught - the individual must recognize and awaken it within themselves by themselves.

And the moment you place your eyes on the ever-radiant glare of humanity in the depth of your heart, all separations would disappear from your field of vision - all barriers would crumble to dust from the fabric of your perception – and what will prevail is a plain, ordinary, sanctifying sense of humanity - only humanity would remain and everything else would turn completely blank - not an object, not a name, not a culture, not a creed, not even a sound - you could see nothing, you could hear nothing, you could feel nothing - all you could comprehend - all you could perceive - all you could realize - is that one fervor - that one fountain of uncorrupted light - your light.

Lo, from the deepest abyss of your soul rises a new, life-giving realization - the realization of love. At that moment, when there is only humanity, you could no longer find yourself in yourself – you could no longer identify yourself with the identity imposed on you by your society - you would be lost in the majestic indivisible, nonsectarian revelation of humanity - all you'd feel is – "there is no time, there is no space, there is only love - there is only kindness" - this is the quintessence of everything that's secular - this is the quintessence of everything that's humane - this is the quintessence of everything that's civilized. Remember, either we are alive and human or we are dead and tribal.

Forget about philosophies - forget about secularism - forget about religion. Why you ask? I'll tell you. After spending most of my life in the observation of religions and beliefs, I have come to one realization - we cannot make a civilized and secular world by talking about religion, we can do so only by speaking of kindness, dreaming of kindness and living of kindness. Let your whole soul be purified with its own streams of kindness, and the whole world will be purified.

# 10. Lost in Definitions

Only the words that you speak with your heart will reach another heart, but those spoken with mere lips will reach nowhere. It's the golden glint of a kind heart that nourishes the fabric of society, not the scorching heat of argumentation. On the odyssey of kindness will the fabric of civilization unfold - not of intellect, not of faith, but of kindness - intellect may help, faith may help, but that's about all.

You see, the heart is the most precious thing people have got, and they won't trade it even for a thousand facts or a thousand hymns, but lend them a kind heart when they need and they'll give you all that is theirs for free. Neither riches nor facts nor doctrines make this world life-worthy - it's kindness that makes it so - and the moment you divide the world with creed, religion and ideology and you insist on those divisions more than you insist on unity, you negate the very conditions that facilitate life.

Unification is life, sectarianism is death - unity is sanity, division is insanity - assimilation is heaven, segregation is hell. But all these are mere words - don't pay too much attention to the words - just remember this, love is life, hate is death. Acceptance, assimilation, unification - all these are manifestations of love.

We have so many words trying to define humanity, but very little of actual humanity - you know why, because we are more obsessed with the means of depiction than the depicted. And it is so, because either we are slave to tradition or we are slave to intellect - neither of which will do if we are to progress as a civilized species - if we are to progress as true sapiens, that is wise beings.

# 11. Pain Delivers Progress

The head is the ladder of progress, but the heart is the one that ought to climb it - place your head beneath your heart and progress will follow. All intellect turns dull when the torch of love is lit - all doctrines turn dismal when the heart is awake with love. It is only when the heart is awake with love that intellect acts as a tool, otherwise intellect does more harm than good.

One person can make a difference, but only if their heart is awake with love, instead of being blinded by the arrogance of intellect or rigidity of faith. When driven by intellect, if someone knocks at our door we judge first and open the door later - when driven by faith, if someone knocks at our door we judge first and open the door later - but when guided by love alone, we open the door first and judge never. And this may lead to heartache at times, but never forget o brave being of character, heartache in love is far better than heartlessness in apathy.

A baby is born when the mother's pain is at its extreme, likewise, a humane world is born only when a handful of bravehearts bear the pain to deliver it out of their sweat and blood. Pain delivers progress. And I'd rather die a martyr than live as a maggot, in the course of delivering that world. The greatest threat to the world is not actually hate, but indifference to hate.

It is this simple - people may not understand your science - people may not understand your scripture - but everyone understands love - it is not merely the supreme language, it is the supreme existence - it is the supreme science as well as the supreme religion.

You don't become religious by memorizing the scripture, whatever that scripture may be - you become religious by loving others without expecting anything in return. This is holiness - this is humaneness - this is secularism - this is humanity. Call it whatever you like - the force is one and the same - the force of love. In religion it's called holiness - in philosophy it's called humanism - in politics it's called secularism.

Different people understand the force as per their own ability - hence they term it differently. Blood though called differently in different parts of the world, carries the same force of life. And this is the quintessence of my life - this is the message behind my existence. Someone asked me, "what's your message to the world" - I replied, "I don't have any message, I am the message."

To live without society is death for me, yet most people call it life. I am but an idea, though I have countless bodies - somewhere it's called Jesus, somewhere Shankara and somewhere else Shams - each vessel may give you a taste of me, but once you recognize the idea beyond the bodies, you'll realize, I live nowhere else but in you. You are an echo of me - I am an echo of you.

The world is but an echo of your voice. And when your voice echoes through the world it'll wash away all prejudicial impurities from the face of this earth. Fear not - you are my fiery sisters and brothers - oppressors will tremble hearing your footsteps and bigots will shiver at the sight of your arrival.

# 12. No Such Thing as Politics

Civilization isn't found, it's built. The law is not going to give you a civilized world - the church is not going to give you a civilized world - the scientific institutes aren't going to give you a civilized world. A civilized world fraught with the sweetness of inclusion and harmony, is to be built by none but ourselves - the ordinary, everyday humans. The point is, we hold that sweetness of inclusion and harmony inside of us, all we have to do is bring it out with our actions, breaking our savage practicality called silence.

We live in a society that mocks involvement as fanaticism and radicalism and accepts silence as practicality and norm. And with such attitude we can never build an actual human civilization, that is a civilization suitable for human living. To be able to build a human civilization what's needed is involvement - but not in a judgmental and anti-establishment sort of way, but in a gentle yet bold and accountable sort of way.

Some people often come and tell me - "you are a scientist, you should stay away from affairs of politics" - I smile and reply, "there is no such thing as affairs of politics, there's only affairs of society - and one who is not involved in the affairs of one's society, is not a human to begin with". Indifference to the troubles of society is not practicality, it's worse than cannibalism, for at least the cannibals don't pretend to be civilized.

Don't get so wrapped up in facts or faith that you forget what it's all about - it's about people. People first, everything else later - people first, science later - people first, religion later - people first, philosophy later - people first, partisanism later. None of our achievements has any meaning, if they don't serve the interest of the people. Achievements devoid of people are of no consequence whatsoever. If your achievements do not improve the lives of the people around, then what's the point of it all!

# 13. Time to Grow Up

There is a difference between growing up and growing old - most people grow old without ever growing up. And the problem with this world is that it's filled with too many old people and very few grown-ups. You see - growing up has nothing to do with physical maturity, it has to do with psychological maturity - and I am not talking about some cockeyed shallow maturity that often people boast about - rather, I am talking about the maturity that destroys all illusion of separation between the self and the other.

Without this maturity no peace is possible on earth. This simple, ordinary maturity of the mind is so rare that traditions across the world have deemed it as a most revered experience, which according to them can only be attained by a saintly soul - and that's where they made the most disastrous mistake of belief - you see - if you declare an experience to be unattainable by ordinary humans, then such an experience has no business existing in the world of ordinary humans - it is only when we consider an experience ordinary - as ordinary as breathing or drinking, can a person live that experience in practice instead of theorizing and speculating over it.

Call it enlightenment, call it nirvana, call it samadhi, call it whatever you want - the fact of the matter is, it's just plain ordinary psychological maturity which is as imperative in the society of humans as oxygen, because without this maturity our fast-growing society of mechanically minded humans will soon die of dehydration.

Awaken that maturity within you my friend, for the society will never ask for you to become mature, despite the fact that it's in dire need of that maturity - society will continue to condition you to be selfish and materially obsessed - awaken the maturity within - be dissolved in your own sunlight - for only then will the osmosis of light and selflessness start in the collective.

Say to yourself - bullets can't penetrate me, fire can't burn me, water can't drown me - I am omnipotent - I am omnipresent. This may sound absolutely stupid, but without such stupidity no feat of remarkable greatness can ever be achieved, especially in a world where complacency and indifference are taken to be sanity and practicality.

# 14. Real Sign of Advancement

The upliftment of the ill-treated must come first, only then can we call ourselves human. You have two choices - either be an inconsequential face amidst the meaningless crowd of practical population, or you can stand up as an utter inconvenience to the established norm, on the side of the voiceless, the helpless, the discriminated and the forgotten.

The child of a poor farmer or a construction worker has as much right to a healthy and happy life, as the child of a billionaire - and till we make it happen, not a single day can go without our involvement to lift our society with our own two hands. This very involvement is the very lifeblood of a functional democracy.

Democracy doesn't mean you leave everything to a bunch of politicians and expect them to take care of everything in your life, that is, in the life of the citizens, yet that's precisely what most people think of democracy to be - a system that frees them from all responsibility. And this lack of responsibility continues to make the disparities of our society more striking. Remember, a democracy that cannot solve the basic issue of inequality isn't worth a penny, no matter how much outward advancement it facilitates. First equality, then everything else, that's the motto for a civilized democracy.

Take India for example. Despite being one of the oldest civilizations and a country with the most affordable, successful space program in the world, not one of the affordable but most affordable (their last moon mission Chandrayaan-II cost less than what it took to make the movie Interstellar), it still suffers from the filthy atrocity of inequality. You see, there's not one but two India, not unlike our America, where one part has more than it needs and another has not even the fundamentals to sustain life. If this is advancement, then I'm afraid it's not the advancement of a living species, but that of a bunch of mechanical morons.

For example, intellectuals like to say that advancement in medical science has increased the average lifespan of the human species, which may be factually correct, but the real picture is not as straight forward as that, because while modern medicine has been a boon to the already privileged, it has done very little for those without the means to afford such advancement. In short, even the very concept of advancement is fraught with disparity in our so-called civilized world.

Till healthcare becomes free through welfare benefits or extremely affordable, to everyone, boasting about the advancements in medicine is like boasting about the features of a Rolls Royce to a poor villager in Africa. Advancement that serves only the privileged is no advancement. Take the COVID19 vaccine from Pfizer and Moderna for example. Both vaccines are now being distributed in most of the privileged countries of the world, including our United States. But what about the unprivileged countries! The answer is, who cares - so long as the rich countries can be vaccinated against the pandemic we can consider the pandemic under control.

And that's the hypocrisy of our world. Whether we consider an advancement a success or not is predicated on how well it serves the privileged population. And with such hypocrisy we have no right to call ourselves human, even if we soon succeed in stepping foot on Mars. To put it simply, industry is not the sign of advancement, equality is.

I have a dream of an akhand prithvi - an undivided earth. I will perish, but the dream will live on through generations to come till it is fully realized. And the first step to achieve this dream is to recognize the issues that sustain the divisions in the first place, be it the divisions in access to the fundamentals of life or the divisions caused by sectarianism, and once we have recognized them then we can set course to solve them.

But mark you, we cannot solve the issues of society by simply pretending to know about the solutions - so we must first accept our ignorance. I haven't met a scientist, who knew everything – I haven't met a doctor, who knew everything – I haven't met a teacher who knew everything - there is nothing wrong in not knowing - in fact, it's by knowing that we don't know can we start to know - that's how we find solutions - that's how we solve problems.

Here's the fact on the matter - solutions require a lot of thinking with a touch of creativity. And chaos is the mother of creativity, order is the mother of rigidity - but here's the dilemma - society can't survive in absolute chaos and on the other hand, society can't progress in absolute order. So, for the society to sustain itself and progress at the same time, there must be a healthy interaction between order and chaos. Remember, every feat of originality is born of chaos, but to make that feat effective in society, a little order is required.

# 15. Gospel of Climate Change

We cannot solve the problems that our ancestors couldn't by thinking and acting like them - and more importantly, we cannot solve the problems that our ancestors created by thinking and acting like them - we must think original and act out of that originality.

Take climate change for example. When our ancestors first tasted the illusive sweetness of industrialization, they couldn't help but jump into the deep end lock, stock and barrel. They had no way of knowing what that industrialization would do to the planet's health. However, soon the scientists started to notice the changes in earth's climate and they immediately began to raise concerns, but almost nobody game a damn - you know why, because the taste of money was too sweet for them to be concerned with anything that required to dial down on the industrial growth that made way for economic prosperity.

And today though we may accept this indifference of our ancestors as mere stupidity, we no longer have the barbarian luxury to walk in their same path. Indifference is convenience but equality is necessity, and sometimes we have to give up our convenience to make way for the necessity. Climate action is one of those fundamental necessities of our time, alongside equality. You know why - because climate inaction in 21st century means a future replete with sickness and homelessness for our children, regardless of whether you are a rich entrepreneur or a common construction worker.

You don't have the right to reproduce, unless you are doing your part to reduce carbon emission. Reproduction is an animal tenet but for it to be a human right, the human must carry out the duties that go along with reproduction, that is to make sure the newborns actually have a healthy world to live in, not one infested with disease and geopolitical conflicts.

You see - a handful of governments signing a so-called agreement to tackle global warming doesn't magically stop climate change - you know why - because to keep our planet from heating up all the people of our planet must do their part as much as possible - the tiniest initiatives, that is, the tiniest effort on the individual's part of giving up certain conveniences to help our planet recover, will go a long way.

For example, ditch the car and ride a bike whenever possible, it not only helps tackle climate change, but also keeps you healthy, because riding a biking is one of the best cardiovascular exercises there is and it dumps zero green house gas into the atmosphere.

Individual responsibility is the only surefire cure for the sicknesses of our society, be it climate change, racism, prejudice or discrimination of any kind. Society beings with the self - when the self is responsible, society is healthy - but when the self is irresponsible, society is bound to fall sick. To put it simply, individual accountability is the cure for a sick society - not law, not religion, not science, but accountability of the individual human, no matter who they are and what they do for living.

The human mind is the greatest force for good in the world, but at the same time, it is also the greatest force for evil in the world. But this evil that we talk about is nothing new or out of the ordinary. What we call evil is actually plain, ordinary animal survival instinct, which still remains the fundamental drive for survival in the jungle.

And the trouble is, we may have left the jungle, but the jungle still lives in us – in the neuroanatomy of our mind. So how do we overpower them, the jungle instincts I mean - and the answer is simple enough, but to practice that answer is the difficult part.

We can overpower the jungle instincts in us by practicing the civilized capacities that we have developed more recently, such as reason, compassion, inclusion and assimilation. It's far too easy to be prejudiced, but we must work on our minds not to be - it's far too easy to be discriminatory, but we must work on our minds not to be - it's far too easy to go bonkers over ideological loyalty, but we must work on our minds not to. Why you ask? Because that's the only way our children can live in a world without the fear of being subjugated in mind or in body.

# 16. Life Beyond Subjugation

Before we were subjugated by the forces of nature, now we are subjugated by society. We give in to every single poppycock demand of the society even at the cost of our own individuality. Then we wonder, why are we so unhappy! I'll tell you why - it's because you try so hard to please the savage whims of society that you forget what you are - you forget what you are really capable of - you try so hard to comply with the demands of your society that you forget to recognize your own abilities. Naturally a society full of second-hand humans keeps producing more second-hand humans to sustain the deplorable tradition of second-handness.

Even the teachers who are supposed to build beings of character, dedicate themselves wholeheartedly to produce a bunch of competitive manikins. They talk most proudly about morals but when it comes to practice, they teach the students the art of competition, selfishness and silence - then they wonder why is there so much inequality and suffering in the world! What a disgusting hypocrisy! I pity these so-called teachers.

And to those teachers who try extremely hard to control their students and keep them quiet in class, I say - if you want quiet in the class, join a monastery of bald-headed corpses. Students don't learn by keeping quiet, they learn by actively engaging in the conversation. So, don't try to control your students. If you are teaching right, you'll be in control.

This is the problem with our world - everybody wants to control everybody else. The teachers want to control their students, the companies want to control their consumers, the governments want to control their citizens, the churches want to control their followers.

Life is like the ocean, the more you try to contain it in your fist, the more it seeps out. Life always finds a way. Paradigms of society may attempt to contain life, but they only fail. However, I am not talking about mere rebelling against society - what I am talking about is taking the society in a humane and healthy direction, which is only possible when you break all barriers - but how do you break those barriers - you do so by simply not letting them control your life.

Norms are necessary to sustain the fabric of society, but not all norms are healthy. Be aware of those norms beyond the society's definition of those norms and then accept only those that do not induce hate, prejudice and discrimination of any kind. Nobody can lay out the map for you to know which norms are healthy, which are unhealthy - you must figure that out for yourself. It is this simple, a norm doesn't have to be logical to exist in a civilized society, it just has to be non-prejudicial. The individual must find their way, only then the world will find its way.

# 17. Either Selfish or Human

Norms don't make a society, character does - norms don't make a person, character does. And when that character is wide awake, no norm can poison the society. The idea of secularism promotes a peaceful co-existence among cultures, but to actually achieve such peaceful co-existence, we must first break our allegiance to our own culture - to our own so-called background. So long as I am unequivocally I, others will always remain others. The I must become a reflection of you, only then can true secularism prevail, only then can true civilization prevail.

And here's the interesting part - when character is wide awake, there is no I, but only potential at work. Potential finds its way when character is wide awake - it finds the way of selflessness, which is not exactly the path of selflessness, but simply the path that leads to the highest fulfillment of the self. The highest fulfillment of the self is when it loses all sense of self in the benefit of others. And the only thing that stands in its way is your own prejudice - your own biases - biases that keep you from being human - biases that keep you from thinking of others more than you think of yourself and your immediate family.

Perception is one big bias till you question everything - life is one big prejudice unless you question everything - starting with yourself. Anybody can question the outside world, but very few can question themselves. And those who do, contribute the most in the development of society. However, I am not talking about being critical of yourself, what I am asking is that you be aware of your impulses, for not all impulses can be considered human, many of them are primitive, animal impulses, which are meant to ensure your self-preservation in the path of survival, not to help you understand reality or build a just and humane society.

Life is founded on the selfish drive for survival - unless you cross that hurdle, you can never become human. You are either selfish or human. If we were living in the jungle along with other animals fighting against the elements, then this hurdle wouldn't have been a hurdle but the true force for existence, but we no longer live with other animals in the animal kingdom, do we!

Let me give you a simple example. If we were living in the jungle, then getting laid as much as possible would be one of our prime priorities, with or without consent, for such an act would ensure the survival of our genes, but in a civilized society there is nothing great about getting laid, animals do that all the time, but laying down oneself for the benefit of others, that's greatness - and more importantly, that's humanity. There's no charity, there's only humanity.

18. **Battle Hymn of The Public**
(The Humanist Sonnet)

## Battle Hymn of The Public
### (The Humanist Sonnet)

Mine eyes have seen the glory,
Of the rising of the Gods.
We are fighting all the worry,
Trampling authority of the frauds.
We are awakening ourselves,
Breaking the spell of tradition.
Finally we are breathing free,
Devoid of all segregation.
We still have our prejudices,
But we no longer bow to them.
Biases may still prevail in us,
No more do we submit to them.
God ain't up there but here in you and me.
Awake, Arise O Mighty Gods to die for the unfree.

# 19. The Real Conquest

Exclusively national concern can no longer solve national problems. To solve problems of our nations, what we need is international concern - international solidarity - international unity. Every idea has to become broad enough to engulf the whole world, only then can it solve the problems of even the tiniest neighborhood of the world. To become broad, to assimilate, to universalize is the ultimate goal of a civilized species. Yet we have been walking in the opposite direction. Instead of broadening ourselves, we've been getting smaller - we've been making ourselves narrower in mind, that is, in spirit.

Each individual must give, in order to live. Each nation must give, in order to live. You must give life to have life - without shallowness, without narrowness - with your arms wide open and heart expanded - the more you give life, the more you'll have life. And whenever you try to keep life imprisoned behind four walls, death will be upon you. So expand my sisters and brothers - expand your hearts – expand your minds - expand your horizons beyond the wildest imaginations of your traditions - and the whole world will become your home.

If you want to conquer something, conquer hearts, not lands - if you want possessions, possess memories, not materials. Only love can conquer hate. When armies try to conquer armies, it only makes savages out of humanity. So the answer to the problems of our world is not more armed intervention, but intervention of the heart. The heart of every single thinking and feeling human must intervene in the matters of the world - we no longer have the luxury to be stuck in our little corner of society, living our life in comfort and security - we must throw all comfort and security overboard and jump into the deep end to solve at least one little problem of our world.

In this work, there is no place for prejudice. Minds that are weak, that are incapable of originality, thrive on prejudice under the banner of religious and cultural identity. And in peddling the illusive supremacy of their religious and cultural identity, they object most persistently to notions of unity and secularism - the very idea of expansion threatens the narrow-minded maggots whose very existential identity is predicated on prejudice. But I say to you, the very condition of life is expansion - and in expansion we'll attain unification - in expansion we'll attain universality.

Therefore, prejudices mustn't be accepted as the norm, even if they happen to be peddled by the chosen leader of your land. If you make way for even one prejudice to go unchallenged, either in the name of faith or nationality, soon you'll have no nation to speak of in a globalizing world. We have arrived at a point of time in history, where there is no place for exclusive national or cultural identity upon the fabric of society. With one hand foster your cultural identity, with another assimilate others - this is the golden principle of progress, both national and global, for the watchwords of a civilized society are reason and inclusion, not rigidity and exclusion.

# BIBLIOGRAPHY

Archer M., (2000), Being Human: The Problem of Agency. Cambridge University Press.

Archer M., (2003), Structure, Agency and the Internal Conversation. Cambridge University Press.

Adolphs R (2003) Cognitive neuroscience of human social behaviour. Nature Rev Neurosci 4: 165–178.

Adolphs R, Tranel D, Damasio AR (2003) Dissociable neural systems for recognizing emotions. Brain Cogn 52: 61–69.

Afton, A. D. (1985). Forced copulation as a reproductive strategy of male lesser scaup: A field test of some predictions. - Behaviour 92, p. 146-167.

Allison T, Puce A, McCarthy G. (2000) Social perception from visual cues: role of the STS region. Trends Cogn Sci 4: 267–278.

Andresen, Jensine, and Robert Forman, eds. Cognitive Models and Spiritual Maps. Bowling Green, Ohio: Imprint Academic, 2000.

Ashbrook, James, and Carol Albright. The Humanizing Brain: Where Religion and Neuroscience Meet. Cleveland, OH: Pilgrim Press, 1997.

Azari, Nina, Janpeter Nickel, Gilbert Wunderlich, Michael Niedeggen, Harald Hefter, Lutz Tellmann, Hans Herzog, Petra Stoerig, Dieter Birnbacher, and Rudiger Seitz. "Neural Correlates of Religious Experience." European Journal of Neuroscience 13, no. 8 (2001)

Agar, N. (2004). Liberal eugenics: In defence of human enhancement. London: Blackwell Publishing.

Alteheld, N., Roessler, G., Vobig, M., & Walter, R. (2004). The retina implant new approach to a visual prosthesis. Biomedizinische Technik, 49(4), 99–103.

Antal, A., Nitsche, M. A., Kincses, T. Z., Kruse, W., Hoffmann, K. P., & Paulus, W. (2004a). Facilitation of visuo-motor learning by transcranial direct current stimulation of the motor and extrastriate visual areas in humans. European Journal of Neuroscience, 19(10), 2888–2892.

Bhat Z, Kumar, S, Bhat H (2015) In vitro meat production. Challenges and benefits over conventional meat production. J Sci Food Agric 14: 241–248

Bernstein R. J., (1967), John Dewey. New York: Washington Square Press.

Bernstein R.J., (1971), Praxis and Action: Contemporary Philosophies of Human Activity. Philadelphia: University of Pennsylvania Press.

Bernstein R.J., (1976), The Restructuring Social and Political Thought.

Bernstein R.J., (1983), Beyond Relativism and Objectivism: Science, Hermeneutics, and Praxis. Philadelphia: University of Pennsylvania Press.

Bernstein R.J., (1986), Philosophical Profiles. Philadelphia: University of Pennsylvania Press.

Bernstein R.J., (1991), New Constellation. Cambridge: MIT Press.

Barash, D. P. (1977). Sociobiology of rape in mallards (Anas platyrhynchos): Responses of the mated male. - Science 197, p. 788-789.

Berger, J. (1986). Wild horses of the great basin: Social competition and population size. - The University of Chicago Press, Chicago.

Birkhead, T. R., Johnson, S. D. & Nettleship, D. N. (1985). Extra-pair matings and mate guarding in the common murre Uria aalge. - Anim. Behav. 33, p. 608-619.

Beauregard, Mario, and Vincent Paquette. "Neural Correlates of a Mystical Experience in Carmelite Nuns." Neuroscience Letters 405, no. 3 (2006)

Benson, Herbert. Timeless Healing: The Power and Biology of Belief. New York: Scribner, 1996

Bogen, J.E.(1995a), 'On the neurophysiology of consciousness: Part I. An overview', Consciousness and Cognition, 4.

Bogen, J.E. (1995b), 'On the neurophysiology of consciousness: Part II. Constraining the semantic problem', Consciousness and Cognition, 4.

Bremner, J. D., R. Soufer, et al. (2001). "Gender differences in cognitive and neural correlates of remembrance of emotional words." Psychopharmacol Bull 35 (3).

Brothers, L. (2002). The social brain: A project for integrating primate behavior and neurophysiology in a new domain. In J. T. Cacioppo et al. (Eds.), Foundations in neuroscience. Cambridge, MA: MIT Press.

Buss, D. D. (2003). Evolutionary Psychology: The New Science of Mind, 2nd ed. New York: Allyn & Bacon.

Buss, D. M. (1989). "Conflict between the sexes: Strategic interference and the evocation of anger and upset." J Pers Soc Psychol 56 (5).

Buss, D. M. (1995). "Psychological sex differences. Origins through sexual selection." Am Psychol 50 (3).

Buss, D. M. (2002). "Review: Human Mate Guarding." Neuro Endocrinol Lett 23 (Suppl 4).

Buss, D. M., and D. P. Schmitt (1993). "Sexual strategies theory: An evolutionary perspective on human mating." Psychol Rev 100 (2).

Blakemore SJ, Decety J (2001) From the perception of action to the understanding of intention. Nature Rev Neurosci 2: 561.

Bruce C, Desimone R, Gross CG (1981) Visual properties of neurons in a polysensory area in superior temporal sulcus of the macaque. J Neurophysiol 46: 369–384.

Buccino G, Vogt S, Ritzl A, Fink GR, Zilles K, Freund HJ, Rizzolatti G (2004) Neural circuits underlying imitation of hand actions: an event related fMRI study. Neuron 42: 323–34.

Colapietro V., (1988), "Human Agency: The Habits of Our Being."

Southern Journal of Philosophy, XXVI, 2, pp. 153-68.

Colapietro V., (1992), "Purpose, Power, and Agency." The Monist, 75, 4 (October) pp. 423-44.

Colapietro V., (2003), "Signs and their vicissitudes: Meanings in excess of consciousness and functionality." Logica, Dialogica, Ideologica, a cure di Susan Petrilli e Patrizia Calefato (Milano: Mimesis), pp. 221-36.

Colapietro V., (2004a), "C. S. Peirce's Reclamation of Teleology." Nature in American Philosophy, ed. Jean De Groot (Washington, D.C.: Catholic University Press of America), pp. 88-108.

Colapietro V., (2004b), "Portrait of a Historicist: An Alternative Reading of Peircean Semiotic." Semiotiche, 2/04 [maggio 2004], pp. 49-68.

Colapietro V., (2006), "Engaged Pluralism: Between Alterity and

Sociality." The Pragmatic Century: Conversations with Richard J. Bernstein (Albany, NY: SUNY Press), pp. 39-68.

Colapietro V., (2009), "Habit, Competence, and Purpose." Forthcoming in The Transactions of the Charles S. Peirce Society. Calder AJ, Keane J, Manes F, Antoun N, Young AW (2000) Impaired recognition and experience of disgust following brain injury. Nature Neurosci 3: 1077–1078.

Carey DP, Perrett DI, Oram MW (1997) Recognizing, understanding and reproducing actions. In: Jeannerod M, Grafman J (eds) Handbook of neuropsychology. Vol. 11: Action and cognition. Elsevier, Amsterdam.

Carr L, Iacoboni M, Dubeau MC, Mazziotta JC, Lenzi GL (2003) Neural mechanisms of empathy in humans: a relay from neural systems for imitation to limbic areas. Proc Natl Acad Sci USA 100: 5497–5502.

Changeux JP, Ricoeur P (1998) La nature et la règle. Odile Jacob, Paris.

Cochin S, Barthelemy C, Roux S, Martineau J (1999) Observation and execution of movement: similarities demonstrated by quantified electroencephalograpy. Eur J Neurosci 11: 1839– 1842.

Chomsky Noam, (2017) Requiem for the American Dream

Chomsky Noam, (2016) Who Rules the World?

Chomsky Noam, (2010) How the World Works

Churchland, P.S. (1986), Neurophilosophy (Cambridge, MA: The MIT Press).

Churchland, P.S. & Ramachandran, V.S. (1993), 'Filling in: Why Dennett is wrong', in Dennett and His Critics:

Demystifying Mind, ed. B. Dahlbom (Oxford: Blackwell Scientific Press).

Churchland, P.S., Ramachandran, V.S. & Sejnowski, T.J. (1994), 'A critique of pure vision', in Large- scale Neuronal Theories of the Brain, ed. C. Koch & J.L. Davis (Cambridge, MA: The MIT Press).

Crick, F. (1994), The Astonishing Hypothesis: The Scientific Search for the Soul (New York: Simon and Schuster).

Crick, F. (1996), 'Visual perception: rivalry and consciousness', Nature, 379.

Crick, F. & Koch, C. (1992), 'The problem of consciousness', Scientific American, 267.

Craig AD (2002) How do you feel? Interoception: the sense of the physiological condition of the body. Nature Rev Neurosci 3: 655–666.

Damasio, A (2003a) Looking for Spinoza. Harcourt Inc. Damasio A (2003b) Feeling of emotion and the self. Ann NY Acad Sci 1001: 253–261.

d'Aquili, Eugene. "Senses of Reality in Science and Religion." Zygon 17, no 4 (1982)

d'Aquili, Eugene. "The Biopsychological Determinants of Religious Ritual Behavior." Zygon 10, no. 1 (1975)

d'Aquili, Eugene. "The Myth-Ritual Complex: A Biogenetic Structural Analysis." Zygon 18, no. 3 (1983)

d'Aquili, Eugene, and Andrew Newberg. The Mystical Mind: Probing the Biology of Religious Experience. Minneapolis: Fortress Press, 1999.

Daly DD. 1958. Ictal affect. Am J Psychiatry.

Damasio, A. (1994) Descartes' Error: Emotion, Reason and the Human Brain. New York, Putnams.

Damasio, A. (1999) The Feeling of What Happens: Body, Emotion and the Making of Consciousness. London, Heinemann.

Darwin, C. (1859) On the Origin of Species by Means of Natural Selection. London, Murray.

Darwin, C. (1871) The Descent of Man and Selection in Relation to Sex. London, John Murray.

Darwin, C. (1872) The Expression of the Emotions in Man and Animals. London, John Murray; also published 1965, Chicago, University of Chicago Press.

Dawkins, M.S. (1987) Minding and mattering. In C. Blakemore and S. Greenfield (eds) Mindwaves. Oxford, Blackwell, 151-60.

Dawkins, R. (1976) The Selfish Gene. Oxford, Oxford University Press; a new edition, with additional material, was published in 1989.

Dawkins, R. (1986) The Blind Watchmaker. London, Longman.

Di Pellegrino G, Fadiga L, Fogassi L, Gallese V, Rizzolatti G (1992) Understanding motor events: A neurophysiological study. Exp Brain Res 91: 176–80.

Deikman, A.J. (2000) A functional approach to mysticism. Journal of Consciousness Studies 7(11-12), 75-91.

Delmonte, M.M. (1987) Personality and meditation. In M. West (ed.) The Psychology of Meditation. Oxford, Clarendon Press, 118-32.

Dennett, D.C. (1987) The Intentional Stance. Cambridge, MA, MIT Press.

Dennett, D.C. (1988) Quining qualia. In A.J. Marcel and E. Bisiach (eds)

Consciousness in Contemporary Science. Oxford, Oxford University Press, 42-77.

Dennett, D.C. (1991) Consciousness Explained. Boston, MA, and London, Little, Brown and Co.

Dennett, D.C. (1995a) Darwin's Dangerous Idea. London, Penguin.

Dennett, D.C. (1995b) The unimagined preposterousness of zombies. Journal of Consciousness Studies 2(4), 322-6.

Dennett, D.C. (1995c) Cog: steps towards consciousness in robots. In T. Metzinger (ed.) Conscious Experience. Thorverton, Devon, Imprint Academic, 471-87.

Dennett, D.C. (1995d) The path not taken. Behavioral and Brain Sciences 18, 252-3; commentary on N. Block, On a confusion about a function of consciousness. Behavioral and Brain Sciences 18, 227.

Dennett, D.C. (1996a) Facing backwards on the problem of consciousness. Journal of Consciousness Studies 3(1), 4-6.

Dennett, D.C. (1996b) Kinds of Minds: Towards an Understanding of Consciousness. London, Weidenfeld & Nicolson.

Dennett, D.C. (1997) An exchange with Daniel Dennett. In J. Searle (ed.) The Mystery of Consciousness. New York, New York Review of Books, 115-19.

Dennett, D.C. (1998) The myth of double transduction. In S.R. Hameroff, A.W. Kaszniak and A. C. Scott (eds) Toward a Science of Consciousness: The Second Tucson Discussions and Debates. Cambridge, MA, MIT Press, 97-107.

Dennett, D.C. (1998b) Brainchildren: Essays on Designing Minds. Cambridge, MA, MIT Press.

Dennett, D.C. (2001) The fantasy of first person science. Debate with D. Chalmers, Northwestern University, Evanston, IL, February 2001.

Dennett, D.C. (2003) Freedom Evolves. New York, Penguin.

Dennett, D.C. and Kinsbourne, M. (1992) Time and the observer: the where and when of consciousness in the brain. Behavioral and Brain Sciences 15, 183-247, including commentaries and authors' responses.

Dewey J., (1911 [1977]), "Epistemological Realism: The Alleged Ubiquity of the Knowledge Relation." Journal of Philosophy, VIII, 20 (September 28, 1911).

Dewhurst, Kenneth, and A. W. Beard. "Sudden Religious Conversions in Temporal Lobe Epilepsy." British Journal of Psychiatry 117 (1970)

Dewhurst K, Beard AW. Sudden religious conversions in temporal lobe epilepsy. 1970 Epilepsy Behav 2003

Devinsky O, Lai G. Spirituality and religion in epilepsy. Epilepsy Behav 2008.

Devinsky, O., Morrell, MJ, Vogt, BA. (1995) 'Contribution of anterior cingulate cortex to behavior', Brain, 118.

Douglas Stone A., Chapter 24, The Indian Comet, in the book Einstein and the Quantum, Princeton University Press, Princeton, New Jersey, 2013.

E. Horvitz, "One Hundred Year Study on Artificial Intelligence: Reflections and Framing," ed: Stanford University, 2014.

Einstein A. (1925). "Quantentheorie des einatomigen idealen Gases". Sitzungsberichte der Preussischen Akademie der Wissenschaften.

Eckhart Meister, Selected Writings

Egidi R., ed. (1999), "Von Wright and 'Dante's Dream': Stages in a Philosophical Pilgrim's Progress", in In Search of a New Humanism: the Philosophy of G.H. von Wright, ed. by R. Egidi, Kluwer, Dordrecht.

Fadiga L, Fogassi L, Pavesi G, Rizzolatti G (1995) Motor facilitation during action observation: a magnetic stimulation study. J Neurophysiol 73: 2608–2611.

Fogassi L, Gallese V, Fadiga L, Rizzolatti G (1998) Neurons responding to the sight of goal directed hand/arm actions in the parietal area PF (7b) of the macaque monkey. Soc Neurosci Abs 24:257.5.

Frith U, Frith CD (2003) Development and neurophysiology of mentalizing. Philos Trans R Soc Lond B Biol Sci 358: 459.

Farah, M.J. (1989), 'The neural basis of mental imagery', Trends in Neurosciences, 10.

Finlay BL, Darlington RB (1995) Linked regularities in the development and evolution of mammalian brains. Science 268.

Freud, S. "The Interpretation of Dreams", 1900

Freud, S. "Selected papers on hysteria and other psychoneuroses" Journal of Nervous and Mental Disease 1909.

Freud, S. "The Origin and Development of Psychoanalysis", 1910

Freud, S. "Psychopathology of everyday life", 1914

Freud, S. "Beyond the Pleasure Principle", 1920

Frith, C.D. & Dolan, R.J. (1997), 'Abnormal beliefs: Delusions and memory', Paper presented at the May,

1997, Harvard Conference on Memory and Belief.

Gay, Volney, ed. Neuroscience and Religion. Plymouth, UK: Lexington Books, 2009.

Gazzaniga, M. S. (1985). The social brain. New York: Basic Books.

Gazzaniga, M.S. (1993), 'Brain mechanisms and conscious experience', Ciba Foundation Symposium, 174.

Geschwind N. "Behavioural changes in temporal lobe epilepsy". Psychol Med. 1979.

Gellhorn, E., Kiely, W.F. "Mystical states of consciousness: neurophysiological and clinical aspects." J Nerv Ment Dis. 1972;154:399-405.

Gilbert SL, Dobyns WB, Lahn BT (2005) Genetic links between brain development and brain evolution. Nat Rev Genet 6.

Gray JA. The Psychology of Fear and Stress. 2nd ed. New York, NY: Cambridge University Press; 1988.

Gloor, P. (1992), 'Amygdala and temporal lobe epilepsy', in The Amygdala: Neurobiological Aspects of Emotion, Memory and Mental Dysfunction, ed J.P. Aggleton (New York: Wiley-Liss).

Greenspan, S. I. and S. G. Shanker (2004). The first idea: How symbols, language, and intelligence evolved from our early primate ancestors to modern humans. Cambridge, MA: Da Capo Press.

Grady, D. (1993), 'The vision thing: Mainly in the brain', Discover, June.

Gallagher HL, Frith CD (2003) Functional imaging of 'theory of mind'. Trends Cogn Sci 7: 77.

Gallese V, Fogassi L, Fadiga L, Rizzolatti G (2002) Action representation and the inferior parietal lobule. In: Prinz W, Hommel B (eds) Attention & Performance XIX. Common mechanisms in perception and action. Oxford University Press, Oxford.

Gallese V, Keysers C, Rizzolatti G (2004) A unifying view of the basis of social cognition. Trends Cogn Sci 8: 396–403.

Gangitano M, Mottaghy FM, Pascual-Leone A (2001) Phase specific modulation of cortical motor output during movement observation. NeuroReport 12: 1489–1492.

Gangitano M, Mottaghy FM, Pascual-Leone A (2004) Modulation of premotor mirror neuron activity during observation of unpredictable grasping movements. Eur J Neurosci 20: 2193– 2202.

Goldman AI, Sripada CS (2004) Simulationist models of face-based emotion recognition. Cognition 94: 193–213.

Grèzes J, Costes N, Decety J (1998) Top-down effect of strategy on the perception of human biological motion: a PET investigation. Cogn Neuropsychol 15: 553–582.

Grèzes J, Armony JL, Rowe J, Passingham RE (2003) Activations related to "mirror" and "canonical" neurones in the human brain: an fMRI study. Neuroimage 18: 928–937.

Gross CG, Rocha-Miranda CE, Bender DB (1972) Visual properties of neurons in the inferotemporal cortex of the macaque. J Neurophysiol 35: 96–111.

Hari R, Forss N, Avikainen S, Kirveskari S, Salenius S, Rizzolatti G (1998) Activation of human primary motor cortex during action observation: a neuromagnetic study.

Proc. Natl Acad Sci USA 95: 15061–15065.

Hardy, G. H. (1940). Ramanujan. Cambridge: Cambridge University Press.

Hall, Daniel, Keith Meador, and Harold Koenig. "Measuring Religiousness in Health Research: Review and Critique." Journal of Religion and Health 47, no. 2 (2008)

Harris, Sam, Jonas Kaplan, Ashley Curiel, Susan Bookheimer, Marco Iacoboni, and Mark Cohen. "The Neural Correlates of Religious and Nonreligious Belief." PLoS One 4, no. 10 (October 1, 2009)

Halgren, E. (1992), 'Emotional neurophysiology of the amygdala within the context of human cognition', in The Amygdala: Neurobiological Aspects of Emotion, Memory and Mental Dysfunction, ed J.P. Aggleton (New York: Wiley-Liss).

Halligan PW, Fink GR, Marshal JC, Vallar G. 2003. Spatial cognition: evidence from visual neglect. Trends Cogn Sci.

Handbook of Emotions, Edited by Michael Lewis, Jeannette M. Haviland-Jones, and Lisa Feldman Barrett, The Guilford Press; 3rd edition (2010).

Haggard, P., Clark, S. and Kalogeras, ]. (2002) Voluntary action and conscious awareness, Nature Neuroscience 5, 382-5. Haggard, P., Newman, C. and Magno, E. (1999) On the perceived time of voluntary actions. British Journal of Psychology 90, 291-303.

Hameroff, S.R. and Penrose, R. (1996) Conscious events as orchestrated space-time selections. Journal of Consciousness Studies 3(1), 36-53; also reprinted in J. Shear (ed.) (1997) Explaining Consciousness-The Hard Problem. Cambridge, MA, MIT Press, 177-95.

Hardcastle, V.G. (2000) How to understand theN in NCC. InT. Metzinger (ed.) Neural Correlates of Consciousness. Cambridge, MA, MIT Press, 259-64.

Harding, D.E. (1961) On Having no Head: Zen and the Re-Discovery of the Obvious. London, Buddhist Society.

Hardy, A. (1979) The Spiritual Nature of Man: A Study of Contemporary Religious Experience. Oxford, Clarendon Press.

Hamad, S. (1990) The symbol grounding problem. Physica D 42, 335-46.

Hamad, S. (2001) No easy way out. The Sciences 41(2), 36-42.

Harre, R. and Gillett, G. (1994) The Discursive Mind. Thousand Oaks, CA, Sage.

Haugeland, J. (ed.) (1997) Mind Design II: Philosophy, Psychology, Artificial

Intelligence. Cambridge, MA, MIT Press.

Hauser, M.D. (2000) Wild Minds: What Animals Really Think. New York, Henry Holt and Co.; London, Penguin.

Hearne, K. (1990) The Dream Machine. Northants, Aquarian.

Hebb, D.O. (1949) The Organization of Behavior. New York, Wiley.

Helmholtz, H.L.F. von (1856-67) Treatise on Physiological Optics.

Hess, EH (1975) "The role of pupil size in communication," Scientific American, 233(5), 110–12.

Heyes, C.M. (1998) Theory of mind in nonhuman primates. Behavioral and Brain Sciences 21, 101-48; with commentaries.

Heyes, C.M. and Galef, B.G. (eds) (1996) Social Learning in Animals: The Roots of Culture. San Diego, CA, Academic Press.

Hilgard, E.R. (1986) Divided Consciousness: Multiple Controls in Human Thought and Action. New York, Wiley.

Hocquette JF (2016) Is in vitro meat the solution for the future? Meat Science 120: 167–176

Hodgson, R. (1891) A case of double consciousness. Proceedings of the Society for Psychical Research 7, 221-58.

Hofstadter, D.R. (1979) Code!, Escher, Bach: An Eternal Golden Braid. London, Penguin.

Hofstadter, D.R. and Dennett, D.C. (eds) (1981) The Mind's I: Fantasies and Reflections on Self and Soul. London, Penguin.

Holland, J. (ed.) (2001) Ecstasy: The Complete Guide: A Comprehensive Look at the Risks and Benefits of

MDMA. Rochester, VT, Park Street Press.

Holmes, D.S. (1987) The influence of meditation versus rest on physiological arousal. In M. West (ed.) The Psychology of Meditation. Oxford, Clarendon Press, 81-103.

Holt, J. (1999) Blindsight in debates about qualia. Journal of Consciousness Studies 6(5), 54-71.

Horgan, J. (1994), 'Can science explain consciousness?', Scientific American, 271.

Holloway RL (1996) Evolution of the human brain. In: Lock A, Peters CR (eds) Handbook of human symbolic evolution. Oxford University Press, Oxford

Iacoboni M, Woods RP, Brass M, Bekkering H, Mazziotta JC, Rizzolatti G (1999) Cortical mechanisms of human imitation. Science 286: 2526–2528.

Iacoboni M, Koski LM, Brass M, Bekkering H, Woods RP, Dubeau MC, Mazziotta JC, Rizzolatti G (2001) Reafferent copies of imitated actions in the right superior temporal cortex. Proc Natl Acad Sci USA 98: 13995–13999.

Jeannerod M (1988) The neural and behavioural organization of goal-directed movements. Clarendon Press, Oxford.

Johnson-Frey SH, Maloof FR, Newman-Norlund R, Farrer C, Inati S, Grafton ST (2003) Actions or hand-objects interactions? Human inferior frontal cortex and action observation. Neuron 39: 1053–1058.

Jackson, F. (1982) Epiphenomenal qualia. Philosophical Quarterly 32, 127-36.

James, W. (1890) The Principles of Psychology (2 volumes). London, Macmillan.

James, W. (1902) The Varieties of Religious Experience: A Study in Human Nature. New York and London, Longmans, Green and Co.

Jansen, K. (2001) Ketamine: Dreams and Realities. Sarasota, FL, Multidisciplinary Association for Psychedelic Studies.

Jay, M. (ed.) (1999) Artificial Paradises: A Drugs Reader. London, Penguin.

Jaynes, J. (1976) The Origin of Consciousness in the Breakdown of the Bicameral Mind. New York, Houghton Mifflin.

Johnson, M.K. and Raye, C.L. (1981) Reality monitoring. Psychological Review 88, 67-85.

Kadim I, Mahgoub O, Baqir S et al. (2015) Cultured meat from muscle stem cells: a review of challenges and prospects. J Integr Agr 14: 222–233

Koski L, Iacoboni M, Dubeau MC, Woods RP, Mazziotta JC (2003) Modulation of cortical activity during different imitative behaviors. J Neurophysiol 89: 460–471.

Krolak-Salmon P, Henaff MA, Isnard J, Tallon-Baudry C, Guenot M, Vighetto A, Bertrand O, Mauguiere F (2003) An attention modulated response to disgust in human ventral anterior insula. Ann Neurol 53: 446–453.

Kandel, E. R. In Search of Memory: The Emergence of a New Science of Mind, W. W. Norton & Company (2007).

Kandel E. R. Schwartz JH, Jessel TM. Principles of neural sciences. New York; McGraw Hill, 2000.

Kanizsa, G. (1979), Organization In Vision (New York: Praeger).

Kaloupek DG, Scott JR, Khatami V. Assessment of coping strategies associated with syncope in blood donors. J Psychosom Res. 1985;29:207-214.

Kanwisher, N. (2001) Neural events and perceptual awareness. Cognition 79, 89-113; also reprinted inS. Dehaene (ed.) The Cognitive Neuroscience of Consciousness. Cambridge, MA, MIT Press, 89-113.

Kapleau, Roshi P. (1980) The Three Pillars of Zen: Teaching, Practice, and Enlightenment (revised edn). New York, Doubleday.

Karn, K. and Hayhoe, M. (2000) Memory representations guide targeting eye movements in a natural task. Visual Cognition 7, 673-703.

Kasamatsu, A. and Hirai, T. (1966) An electroencephalographic study on the Zen meditation (zazen). Folia Psychiatrica et Neurologica Japonica 20, 315-36.

Kaiserman-Abramof, I. R., Graybiel, A. M., & Nauta, W. J. (1980). The thalamic projection to cortical area 17 in a congenitally anophthalmic mouse strain. Neuroscience, 5, 41–52.

Kanold, P. O., Kara, P., Reid, R. C., & Shatz, C. J. (2003). Role of subplate neurons in functional maturation of visual cortical columns. Science, 301, 521–525.

Kennedy, H., & Dehay, C. (1988). Functional implications of the anatomical organization of the callosal projections of visual areas V1 and V2 in the macaque monkey. Behav. Brain Res., 29, 225–236.

Kentridge, R.W. and Heywood, C.A. (1999) The status of blindsight. Journal of Consciousness Studies 6(5), 3-11.

Kihlstrom, J.F. (1996) Perception without awareness of what is perceived, learning without awareness of what is learned. In M. Velmans (ed.) The Science of Consciousness. London, Routledge, 23-46.

Kollerstrom, N. (1999) The path of Halley's comet, and Newton's late apprehension of the law of gravity. Annals of Science 56, 331-56.

Kosslyn, S.M. (1980) Image and Mind. Cambridge, MA, Harvard University Press.

Kosslyn, S.M. (1988) Aspects of a cognitive neuroscience of mental imagery. Science 240, 1621-6.

Kinsbourne, M. (1995), 'The intralaminar thalamic nucleii', Consciousness and Cognition, 4.

Kinross, P. "Ataturk: The Rebirth of a Nation", 1964

Kjaer, Troels, Camilla Bertelsen, Paola Piccini, David Brooks, Jorgen Alving, and Hans Lou. "Increased Dopamine Tone during Meditation- Induced Change of Consciousness." Cognitive Brain Research 13, no. 2 (April 2002)

Kölmel HW. 1985. Complex visual hallucinations in the hemianopic field. J Neurol Neurosurg Psychiatry.

Koenig, Harold. "Research on Religion, Spirituality, and Mental Health: A Review." Canadian Journal of Psychiatry 54, no. 5 (May 2009)

Koenig, Harold, ed. Handbook of Religion and Mental Health. San Diego, CA: Academic Press, 1998

Kraepelin E. Psychiatry: A Textbook for Students and Physicians. New York, NY: Science History Publications; 1990.

Lauglin, Charles, John McManus, and Eugene d'Aquili. Brain, Symbol, and Experience. 2nd ed. New York: Columbia University Press, 1992

Lakoff, G. and M. Johnson (1999). Philosophy in the flesh. Basic Books: New York.

LeDoux, J. E. (1996). The emotional brain. New York: Simon & Schuster.

LeDoux, J.E. (1992), 'Emotion and the amygdala', in The Amygdala: Neurobiological Aspects of Emo- tion, Memory and Mental Dysfunction, ed J.P. Aggleton (New York: Wiley-Liss).

Levin, D.T. and Simons, D.J. (1997) Failure to detect changes to attended objects in motion pictures. Psychonomic Bulletin and Review 4, 501-6.

Levine,J. (1983) Materialism and qualia: the explanatory gap. Pacific Philosophical Quarterly 64, 354-61.

Levine,J. (2001) Purple Haze: The Puzzle of Consciousness. New York, Oxford University Press. Levine, S. (1979) A Gradual Awakening. New York, Doubleday.

Levinson, B.W. (1965) States of awareness during general anaesthesia.

British Journal of Anaesthesia 37, 544-6.

Lewicki, P., Czyzewska, M. and Hoffman, H. (1987) Unconscious acquisition of complex procedural knowledge. Journal of Experimental Psychology: Learning, Memory and Cognition 13, 523-30.

Lewicki, P., Hill, T. and Bizot, E. (1988) Acquisition of procedural knowledge about a pattern of stimuli that cannot be articulated. Cognitive Psychology 20, 24-37.

Lewicki, P., Hill, T. and Czyzewska, M. (1992) Nonconscious acquisition of information. American Psychologist 47, 796-801.

Mango A. "Ataturk: The Biography of the Founder of Modern Turkey", 1963

Manthey S, Schubotz RI, von Cramon DY (2003). Premotor cortex in observing erroneous action: an fMRI study. Brain Res Cogn Brain Res 15: 296–307.

Mesulam MM, Mufson EJ (1982) Insula of the old world monkey. III: Efferent cortical output and comments on function. J Comp Neurol 212: 38–52.

Naskar, Abhijit. "Homo: A Brief History of Consciousness", 2015

Naskar, Abhijit. "What is Mind?", 2016

Naskar, Abhijit. "Love, God & Neurons: Memoir of A Scientist who found himself by getting lost", 2016

Naskar, Abhijit. "Principia Humanitas", 2017

Naskar, Abhijit. "We Are All Black: A Treatise on Racism", 2017

Naskar, Abhijit. "Either Civilized or Phobic: A Treatise on Homosexuality", 2017

Naskar, Abhijit. "I Am The Thread: My Mission", 2017

Naskar, Abhijit. "The Bengal Tigress: A Treatise on Gender Equality", 2017

Naskar, Abhijit. "Morality Absolute", 2017

Naskar, Abhijit. "Build Bridges not Walls: In the name of Americana", 2018

Naskar, Abhijit. "Fabric of Humanity", 2018

Naskar, Abhijit. "Lives To Serve Before I Sleep", 2019

Naskar, Abhijit. "Citizens of Peace: Beyond the Savagery of Sovereignty", 2019

Naskar, Abhijit. "The Constitution of The United Peoples of Earth", 2019

Naskar, Abhijit. "Neurons Giveth, Neurons Taketh Away | Abhijit Naskar | TEDxIIMRanchi", 2019 https://www.youtube.com/watch?v=BNX-Q0ySm80

Naskar, Abhijit. "Mission Reality", 2019

Naskar, Abhijit. "Operation Justice: To Make A Society That Needs No Law", 2019

Naskar, Abhijit. "Every Generation Needs Caretakers: The Gospel of Patriotism", 2020

Naskar, Abhijit. "Revolution Indomable", 2020

Naskar, Abhijit. "Servitude is Sanctitude", 2020

Newberg, Andrew, and Jeremy Iversen. "The Neural Basis of the Complex Mental Task of Meditation: Neurotransmitter and Neurochemical Considerations." Medical Hypotheses 61, no. 2 (2003).

Newberg, Andrew. "How God Changes Your Brain: An Introduction to Jewish Neurotheology", CCAR

Journal: The Reform Jewish Quarterly, Winter 2016.

Newberg, Andrew, and Stephanie Newberg. "A Neuropsychological Perspective on Spiritual Development." In Handbook of Spiritual Development in Childhood and Adolescence, edited by Eugene Roehlkepartain, Pamela King, Linda Wagener, and Peter Benson. London: Sage Publications, Inc., 2005

Newberg, Andrew. "The Neurotheology Link An Intersection Between Spirituality and Health", Alternative and Complimentary Therapies, Vol 21 No 1, February 2015.

Newberg, Andrew, Nancy Wintering, Dharma Khalsa, Hannah Roggenkamp, and Mark Waldman. "Meditation Effects on Cognitive Function and Cerebral Blood Flow in Subjects with Memory Loss: A Preliminary Study." Journal of Alzheimer's Disease 20, no. 2 (2010)

Nash, M. (1995), 'Glimpses of the mind', Time.

Nesse RM. Proximate and evolutionary studies of anxiety, stress and depression: synergy at the interface. Neurosci Biobehav Rev. 1999;23:895-903.

Nicolelis, Miguel. (2011) "Beyond Boundaries: The New Neuroscience of Connecting Brains with Machines--- and How It Will Change Our Lives", Times Books

O'Hara, K. and Scutt, T. (1996) There is no hard problem of consciousness. Journal of Consciousness Studies 3(4), 290-302, reprinted in J. Shear (ed.) (1997) Explaining Consciousness. Cambridge, MA, MIT Press, 69-82.

O'Regan, J.K. (1992) Solving the "real" mysteries of visual perception: the world as an outside memory. Canadian Journal of Psychology 46, 461-88.

O'Regan, J.K. and Noe, A. (2001) A sensorimotor account of vision and visual consciousness. Behavioral and Brain Sciences 24(5), 883-917.

O'Regan, J.K., Rensink, R.A. and Clark,].]. (1999) Change-blindness as a result of "mudsplashes." Nature 398, 34.

Ornstein, R.E. (1977) The Psychology of Consciousness (2nd edn). New York, Harcourt.

Ornstein, R.E. (1986) The Psychology of Consciousness (3rd edn). New York, Pehguin.

Ornstein, R.E. (1992) The Evolution of Consciousness. New York, Touchstone.

Penfield W, Faulk ME (1955) The insula: further observations on its function. Brain 78: 445– 470.

Penrose, R. (1994), Shadows of the Mind (Oxford: Oxford University Press).

Penrose, R. (1989), The Emperor's New Mind: Concerning Computers, Minds and The Laws of Physics (Oxford: Oxford University Press).

Persinger, "'I would kill in God's name' role of sex, weekly church attendance, report of a religious experience and limbic lability" Perceptual and Motor Skills 1997.

Persinger "Experimental simulation of the God experience" Neurotheology 2003.

Persinger, M. A. (1993b). Personality changes following brain injury as a grief response to the loss of sense of self: Phenomenological themes as indices of local lability and neurocognitive restructuring as psycho- therapy. Psychological Reports, 72

Persinger, Corradini, Clement, Keaney, et al "Neurotheology and its convergence with neuroquantology" NeuroQuantology 2010.

Persinger, Koren and St-Pierre "The electromagnetic induction of mystical and altered states within the laboratory" Journal of Consciousness Exploration and Research 2010.

Persinger "Case report: A prototypical spontaneous 'sensed presence' of a sentient being and concomitant electroencephalographic activity in the clinical laboratory" Neurocase 2008.

Persinger and Saroka "Potential production of Hughlings Jackson's "parasitic consciousness" by physiologically-patterned weak transcerebral magnetic fields: QEEG and source localization" Epilepsy & Behavior 28 (2013).

Persinger. "The neuropsychiatry of paranormal experiences". J Neuropsychiatry Clin Neurosci 2001.

Persinger. "Neuropsychological bases of god beliefs", New York: Praeger, 1987

Persinger. "Temporal lobe epileptic signs and correlative behaviors displayed by normal populations", Journal of General Psychology, 1986

Perry BD, Pollard R. Homeostasis, stress, trauma, and adaptation. A neurodevelopmental view of childhood trauma. Child Adolesc Psychiatr Clin N Am. 1998;7:33.

Pinker Steven, "Is the world getting better or worse? A look at the numbers", Ted Talks, 2018

Paré, D. & Llinás, R. (1995), 'Conscious and preconscious processes as seen from the standpoint of sleep-waking cycle neurophysiology', Neuropsychologia, 33.

P. S. de Laplace. Essai Philosophique sur les Probabilites [1814], in Academy des Sciences, Oeuvres Complotes de Laplace, Vol. 7, Gauthier-Villars, Paris (1886).

Perrett DI, Harries MH, Bevan R, Thomas S, Benson PJ, Mistlin AJ, Chitty AJ, Hietanen JK, Ortega JE (1989) Frameworks of analysis for the neural representation of animate objects and actions. J Exp Bio 146: 87–113.

Phillips ML, Young AW, Senior C, Brammer M, Andrew C, Calder AJ, Bullmore ET, Perrett DI, Rowland D, Williams SC, Gray JA, David AS (1997) A specific neural substrate for perceiving facial expressions of disgust. Nature 389: 495–498.

Phillips ML, Young AW, Scott SK, Calder AJ, Andrew C, Giampietro V, Williams SC, Bullmore ET, Brammer M, Gray JA (1998) Neural responses to facial and vocal expressions of fear and disgust. Proc R Soc Lond B Biol Sci 265: 1809–1817.

Puce A, Perrett D (2003) Electrophysiological and brain imaging of biological motion. Philosoph Trans Royal Soc Lond, Series B, 358: 435–445.

Ramachandran VS. Behavioral and magnetoencephalographic correlates of plasticity in the adult human brain. Proc Natl Acad Sci USA 1993; 90: 10413–20.

Ramachandran VS. Phantom limbs, neglect syndromes, repressed memories, and Freudian psychology. Int Rev Neurobiol 1994; 37: 291–333.

Ramachandran VS. Plasticity and functional recovery in neurology. Clin Med 2005; 5: 368–73.

Ramachandran VS, Hirstein W. The perception of phantom limbs. The D. O. Hebb lecture. Brain 1998; 121: 1603–30.

Ramachandran VS, Rogers-Ramachandran D, Cobb S. Touching the phantom limb. Nature 1995; 377: 489–90.

Ramachandran VS, Rogers-Ramachandran D. Phantom limbs and neural plasticity. Arch Neurol 2000; 57: 317–20.

Ramachandran VS, Rogers-Ramachandran D. It's all done with mirrors. Sci Am Mind 2007; 18: 16–9.

Ramachandran VS, Rogers-Ramachandran D. Sensations referred to a patient's phantom arm from another subjects intact arm: perceptual correlates of mirror neurons. Med Hypotheses 2008; 70: 1233–4.

Ramachandran VS, Rogers-Ramachandran D, Stewart M. Perceptual correlates of massive cortical reorganization. Science 1992; 258: 1159–60.

Rizzolatti G, Craighero L (2004) The mirror-neuron system. Annu Rev Neurosci 27: 169–192.

Rizzolatti G, Fogassi L, Gallese V (2001) Neurophysiological mechanisms underlying the understanding and imitation of action. Nature Rev Neurosci 2:661–670.

Rock I, Victor J. Vision and touch: an experimentally created conflict between the two senses. Science 1964; 143: 594–6.

Rose'n B, Lundborg G. Training with a mirror in rehabilitation of the hand. Scand J Plast Reconstr Surg Hand Surg 2005; 39: 104–8.

Royet JP, Plailly J, Delon-Martin C, Kareken DA, Segebarth C (2003) fMRI of emotional responses to odors: influence of hedonic valence and judgment, handedness, and gender. Neuroimage 20: 713–728.

Rozin R Haidt J and McCauley CR (2000) Disgust. In: Lewis M, Haviland-Jones JM (eds) Handbook of Emotion. 2nd Edition. Guilford Press, New York, pp 637–653.

Saxe R, Carey S, Kanwisher N (2004) Understanding other minds: linking developmental psychology and functional neuroimaging. Annu Rev Psychol 55: 87–124.

S. J. Russell and P. Norvig, Artificial intelligence: a modern approach (3rd edition): Prentice Hall, 2009.

Schienle A, Stark R, Walter B, Blecker C, Ott U, Kirsch P, Sammer G, Vaitl D (2002) The insula is not specifically involved in disgust processing: an fMRI study. Neuroreport 13: 2023–2026.

Showers MJC, Lauer EW (1961) Somatovisceral motor patterns in the insula. J Comp Neurol 117: 107–115.

Singer T, Seymour B, O'Doherty J, Kaube H, Dolan RJ, Frith CD (2004) Empathy for pain involves the affective but not the sensory components of pain. Science 303: 1157–1162.

Smith A (1759) The theory of moral sentiments (ed. 1976). Clarendon Press, Oxford.

S. N. Bose (1924). "Plancks Gesetz und Lichtquantenhypothese". Zeitschrift für Physik. 26 (1): 178–181.

Sprengelmeyer R, Rausch M, Eysel UT, Przuntek H (1998) Neural structures associated with recognition of facial expressions of basic emotions Proc R Soc Lond B Biol Sci 265: 1927–1931.

Strafella AP, Paus T (2000) Modulation of cortical excitability during action observation: a transcranial magnetic stimulation study. NeuroReport 11: 2289–2292.

Simonsen R (2015) Eating for the future: veganism and the challenge of in vitro meat. In: Stapleton P, Byers A (Hg). Biopolitics and utopia. Palgrave Macmillan, New York (2015), S 167–190

Tanaka K (1996) Inferotemporal cortex and object vision. Ann Rev Neurosci. 19: 109–140.

Tesla N. "My Inventions", 1919

T. R. Society, "Machine learning: the power and promise of computers that learn by example," ed. The Royal Society, 2017.

Tomasello M, Call J (1997) Primate cognition. Oxford University Press, Oxford.

Tremblay C, Robert M, Pascual-Leone A, Lepore F, Nguyen DK, Carmant L, Bouthillier A, Theoret H (2004) Action observation and execution: intracranial recordings in a human subject. Neurology. 63: 937–938.

Umilta MA, Kohler E, Gallese V, Fogassi L, Fadiga L, Keysers C, Rizzolatti G (2001) "I know what you are doing": a neurophysiological study. Neuron 32: 91–101.

Von Wright G.H., (1963), Norm and Action. A Logical Inquiry, Routledge & Kegan Paul, London.

Von Wright G.H., (1976), "Determinism and the Study of Man", in Essays on Explanation and Understanding, ed. by J. Manninen and R. Tuomela, Reidel, Dordrecht.

Von Wright G.H., (1977), "What is Humanism?", The Lindlay Lecture, University of Arkansas, Lawrence, Kansas.

Von Wright G.H., (1979), "Humanism and the Humanities", in Philosophy and Grammar, ed. by S. Kanger and S. Öhman, Reidel, Dordrecht, pp. 1-16. Reprinted in von Wright (1993).

Von Wright G.H., (1980), Freedom and Determination, North-Holland Publishing Co., Amsterdam.

Von Wright G.H., (1985), Of Human Freedom, The Tanner Lectures on Human Values,

Vol. VI, ed. by S. M. McMurrin, University of Utah Press, Salt Lake City, pp. 107-70. Reprinted in von Wright (1998).

Von Wright G.H., (1993), The Tree of Knowledge and Other Essays, Brill, Leiden.

Von Wright G.H., (1997), "Progress: Fact and Fiction", in The Idea of Progress, ed. by A. Burgen et al., W. de Gruyter, Berlin, pp. 1-18.

Von Wright G.H., (1998), In the Shadow of Descartes: Essays in the Philosophy of Mind, Kluwer, Dordrecht.